How Does Your Garden Grow Mr. McDoogle?

Written and Illustrated By:

Marie Whitton

For My Husband
Greg

For My Children
Gregory, Ann-Marie &
Kimberly

For My
Grandchildren

"Hello Mr. McDoogle", we did say,
What a beautiful Spring day.
How does your garden grow?
To us - will you show?
Please, about your garden do tell,
Will you have vegetables to sell?

Tool Shed

WELCOME TO
MR. McDOOGLE'S
GARDEN

Tool Shed

Here is a great place under the sun,
Trees - there are none.
Pick up those rocks,
Put them in a box.

Here is where the plants will grow,
He takes out the tools and makes a row.
He needs the shovel, the rake and hoe,
To sow.

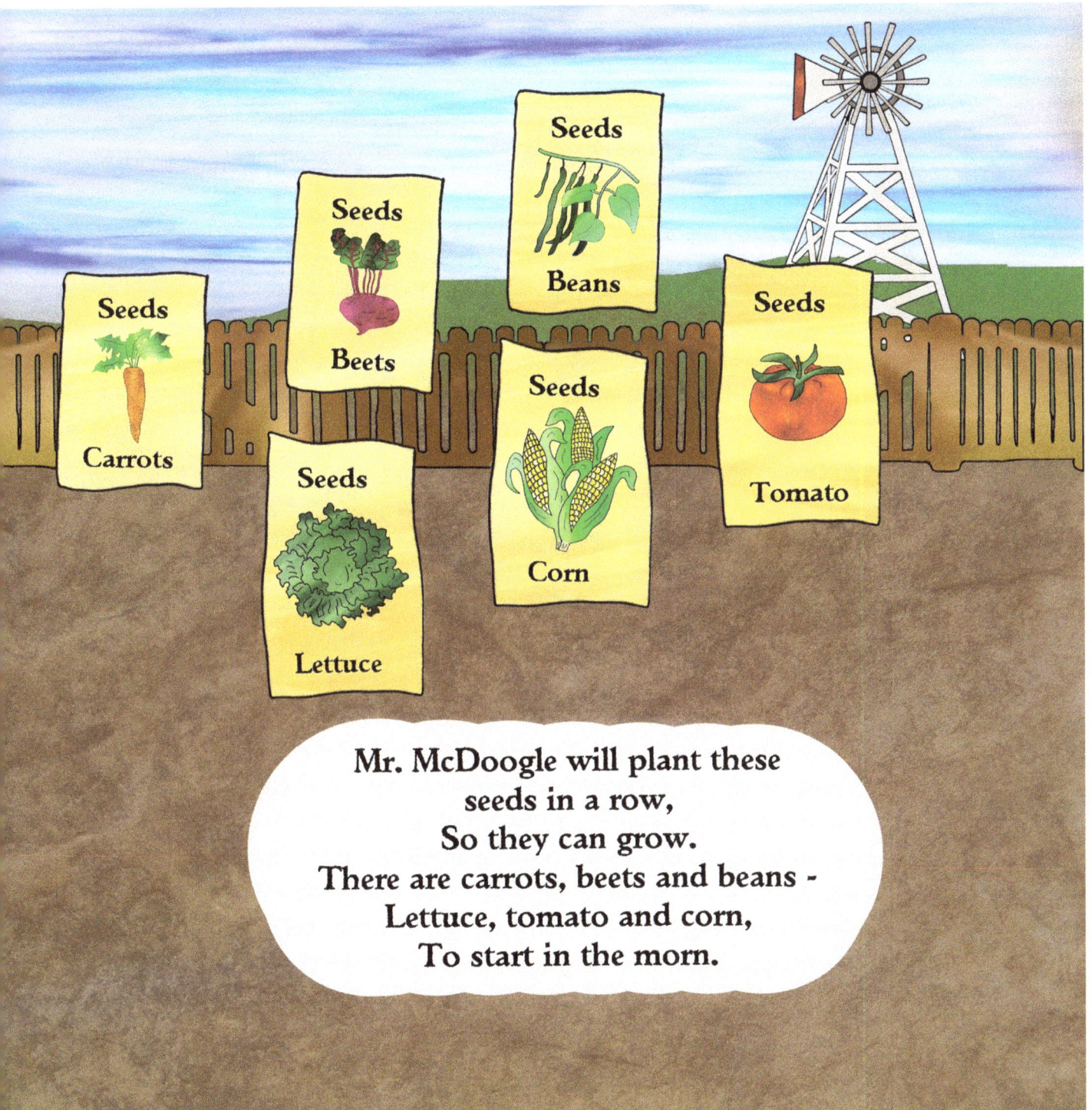

Seeds
Carrots

Seeds
Beets

Seeds
Beans

Seeds
Tomato

Seeds
Lettuce

Seeds
Corn

Mr. McDoogle will plant these
seeds in a row,
So they can grow.
There are carrots, beets and beans -
Lettuce, tomato and corn,
To start in the morn.

Corn

Tomato

Lettuce

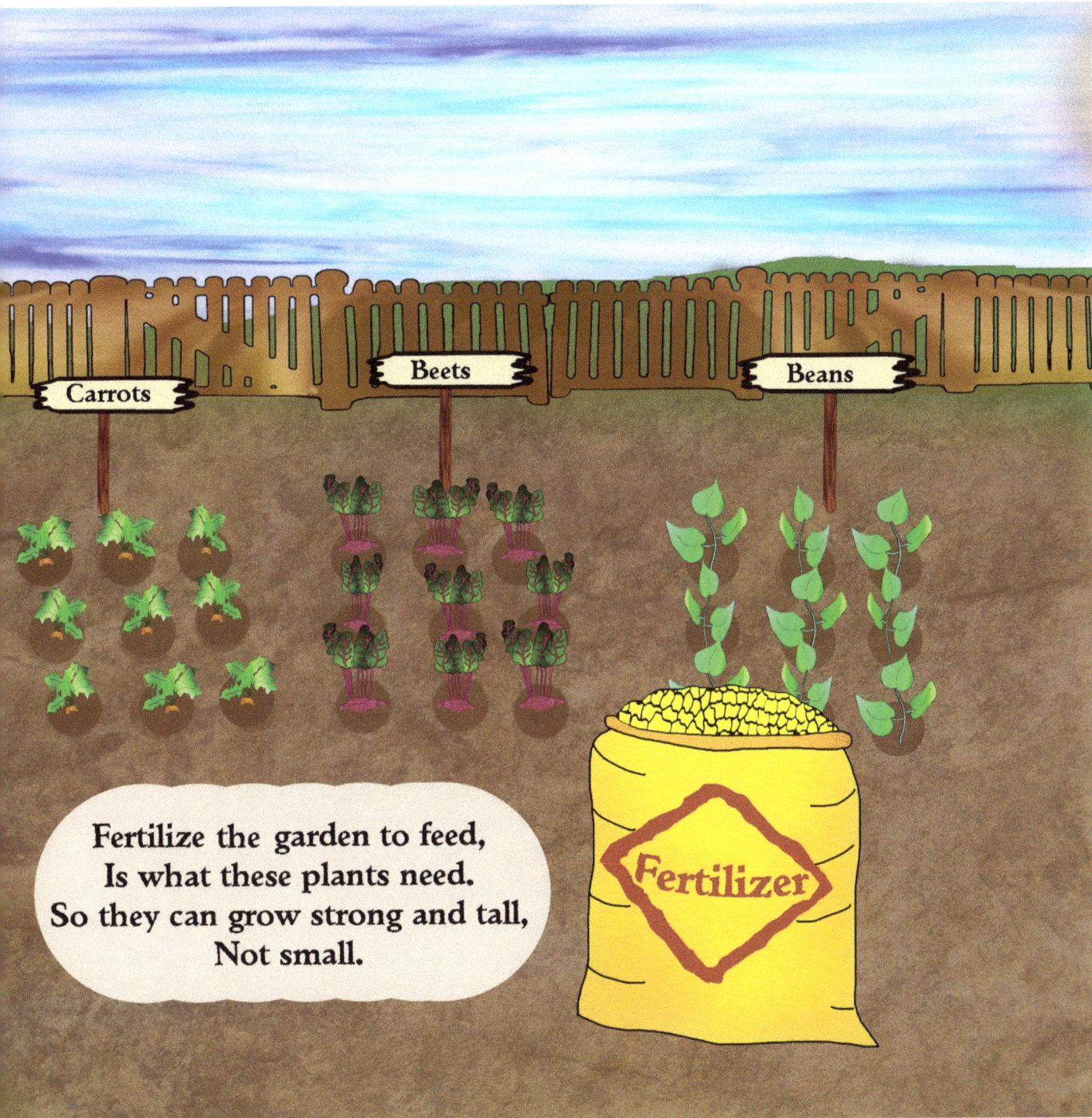

Carrots

Beets

Beans

Fertilize the garden to feed,
Is what these plants need.
So they can grow strong and tall,
Not small.

Fertilizer

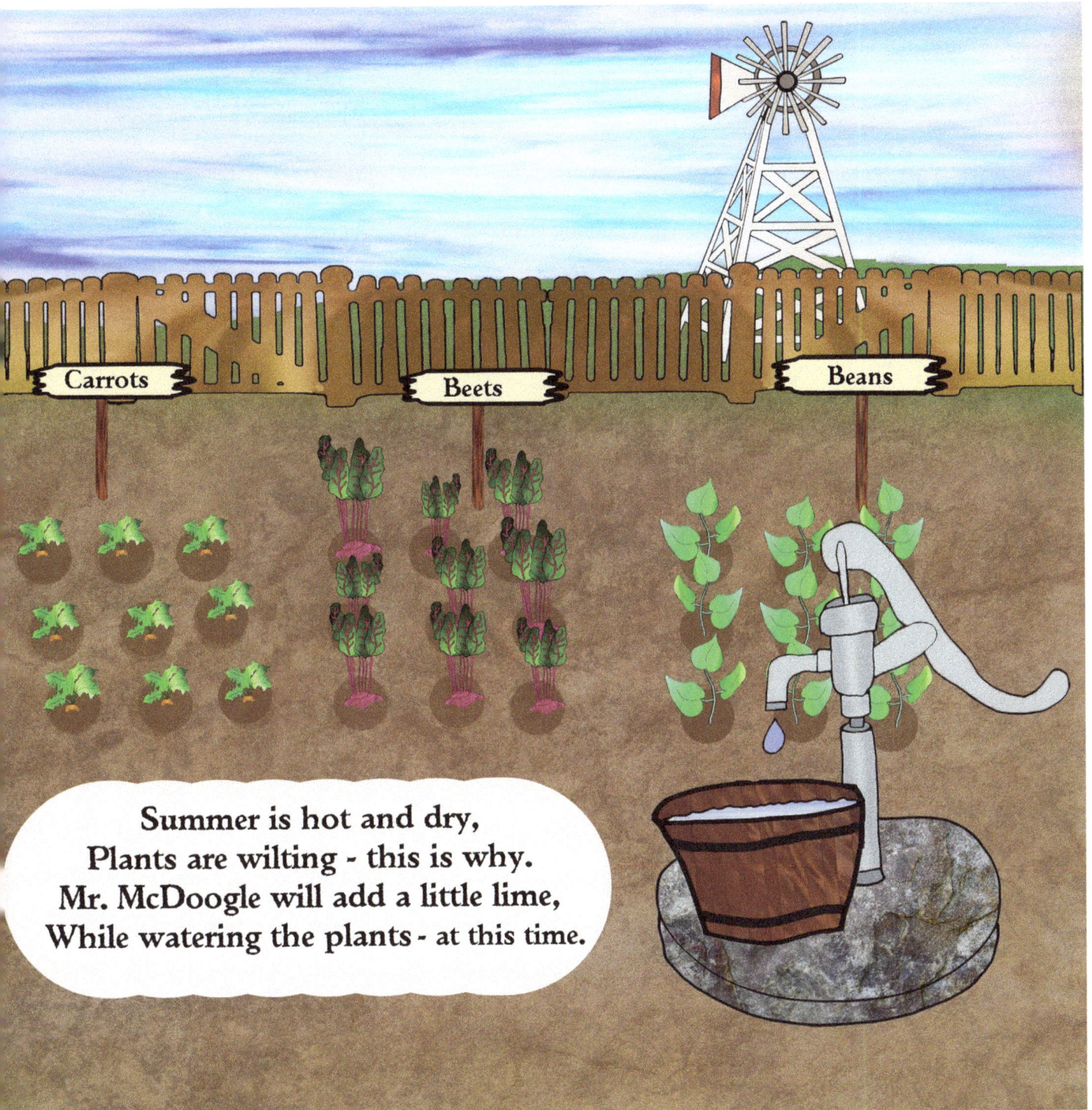

Carrots

Beets

Beans

Summer is hot and dry,
Plants are wilting - this is why.
Mr. McDoogle will add a little lime,
While watering the plants - at this time.

Pollinating a flower by that bee,
This is what we see.
For a vegetable to grow,
This is the way it will go.

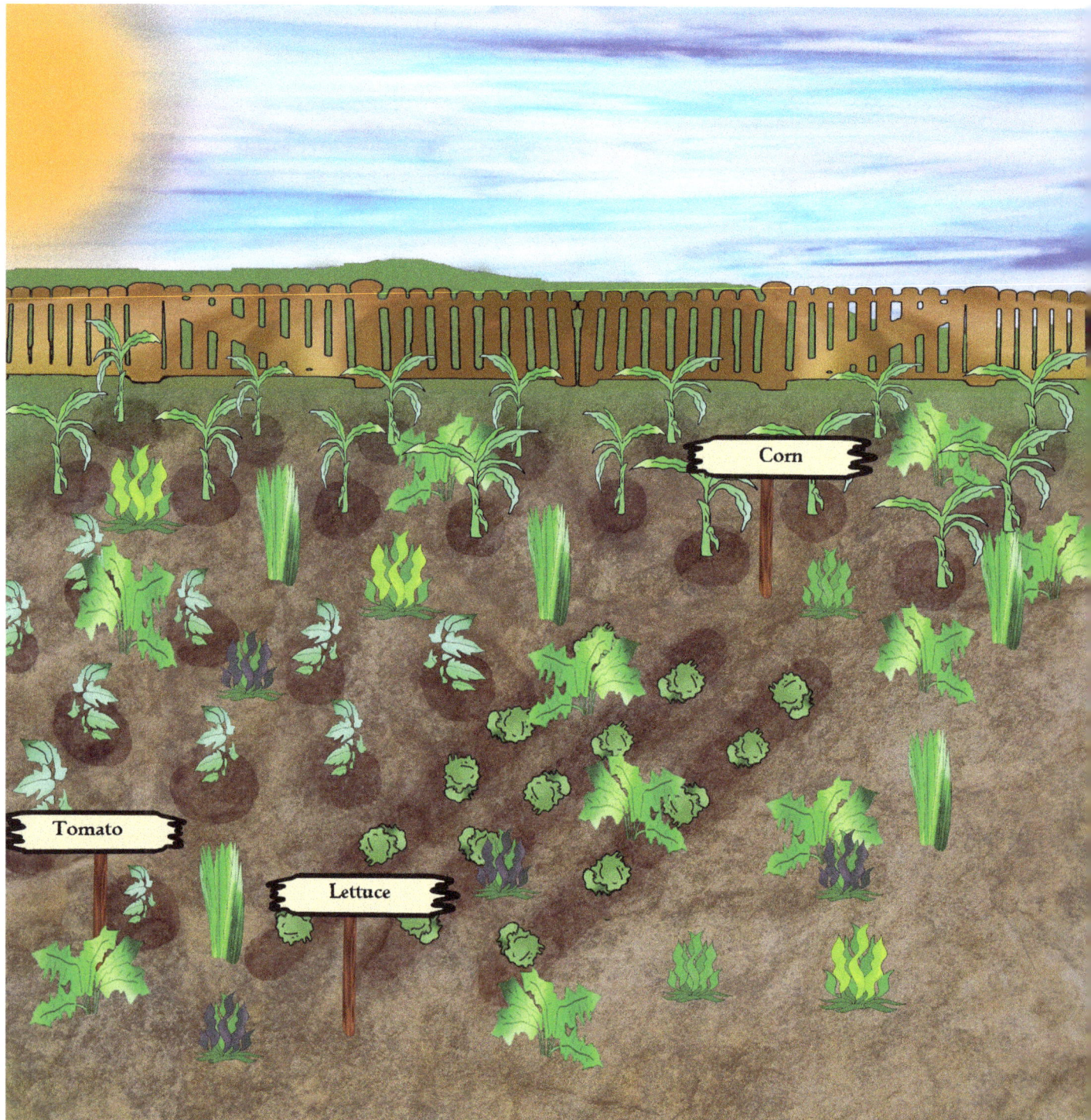

Corn

Tomato

Lettuce

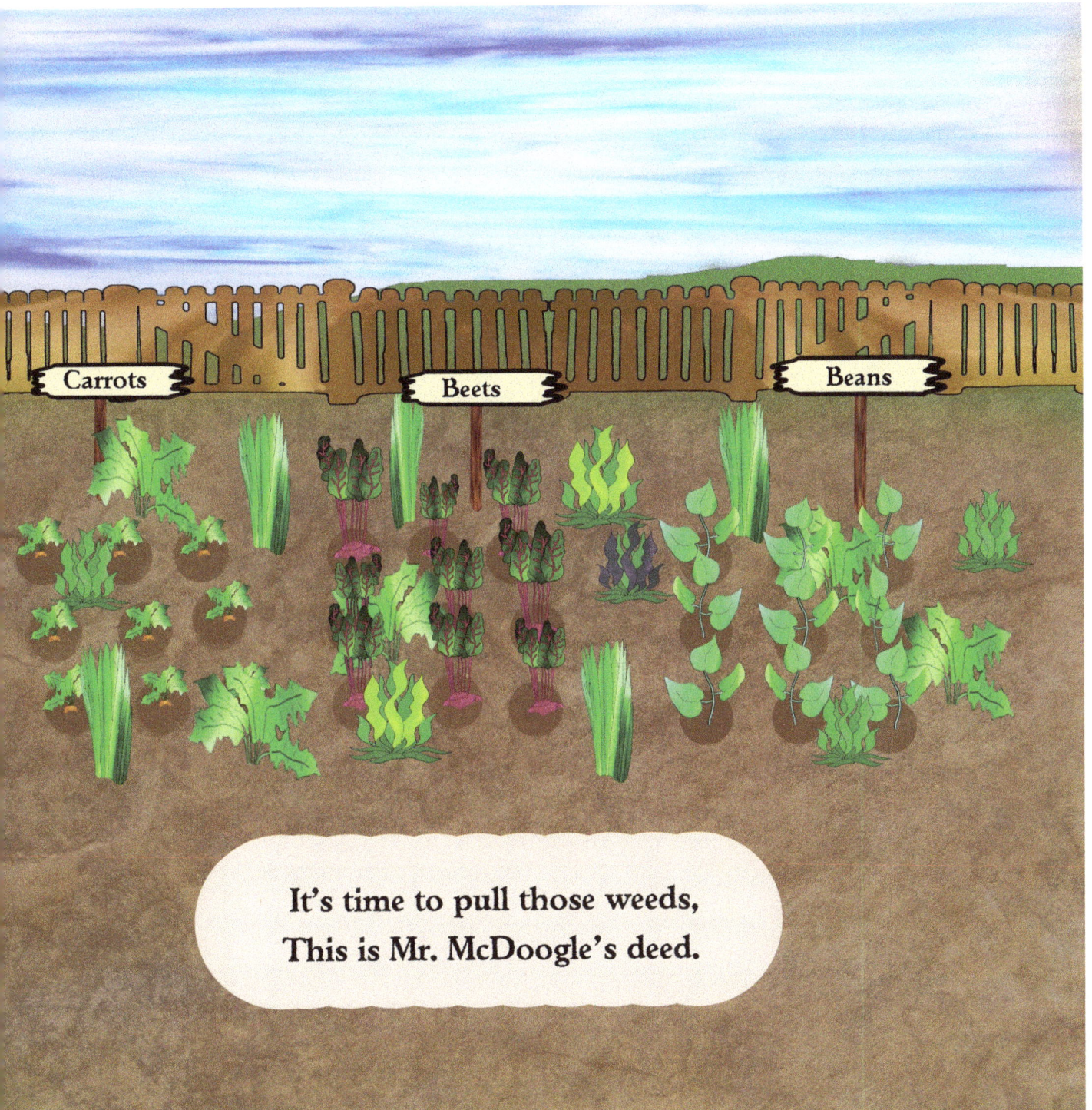

Carrots Beets Beans

It's time to pull those weeds,
This is Mr. McDoogle's deed.

Taking over are the crows,
Mr. McDoogle takes out the scarecrows.
The birds, he has to chase,
Get rid of them - from this place.

Carrots

Beets

Beans

Who left the gate open?

Bunnies started to munch,
A whole bunch.
Don't stay,
Go away.

Corn

Tomato

Lettuce

Carrots

Beets

Beans

Look at the garden - how it did grow,
Mr. McDoogle can reap the crops that
he did sow.

Before the first frost and now in the fall,
Ripened vegetables - he harvested them all.
The beets and carrots he will pull,
Until the basket is full.
Lettuce, tomatoes, corn and beans he will pick,
Click-a-ty click.

To market to sell,
To us he did tell.
Tomatoes, beets and corn to buy,
To take home and try.

Farmer's Market

Beans $2./lb
Beets $3./lb
Corn $4./lb
Carrots $2.50/lb
Tomato $4./lb
Lettuce $2./lb

9 780578 477770